Your Money Day

Informed Choice

Build, manage and protect your wealth

Informed Choice is a leading firm of Chartered Financial Planners, working with individuals, trustees and business owners to build, manage and protect their wealth.

We were named IFA of the Year at the Money Marketing Financial Services Awards 2010. This is a prestigious award recognised in the financial services profession as a significant achievement.

Our highly qualified and experienced team of Financial Planners use their knowledge and skill to deliver impartial and unbiased financial advice to our clients.

As a firm of Chartered Financial Planners, we have satisfied rigorous criteria relating to professional qualifications and ethical good practice. You can be confident that you will be dealing with a leading firm wholly committed to providing the best possible advice, service and support.

Find out more about us at www.icl-ifa.co.uk or on Twitter @informedchoice.

Your Money Day

One day to take control of your finances

Martin Bamford (@martinbamford)
Nick Bamford (@nickbamford)
Andrew Neligan (@andrewneligan)

Informed Choice Ltd

Sundial House, 20 High Street
Cranleigh, Surrey GU6 8AE
Tel: +44 (0)1483 274566
Fax: +44 (0)1483 274640

Website: www.icl-ifa.co.uk

Your Money Day: One day to take control of your finances (paperback edition)

ISBN: 978-1-291-53457-3

First published in Great Britain in 2013

© Informed Choice Ltd 2013

All rights reserved. No part of this publication may be reproduced, stored in a retrieval system, or transmitted in any form or by any means, electronic, mechanical, photocopying, recording or otherwise, without either the prior written permission of the Publishers or a licence permitting restricted copying in the United Kingdom issued by the Copyright Licensing Agency Ltd.

This book may not be lent, resold, hired out or otherwise disposed of by way of trade in any form or binding or cover other than that in which it is published, without the prior consent of the Publishers.

Typeset in 10pt Bookman Old Style

About the authors

Martin Bamford

Martin is a Chartered Financial Planner and published personal finance author.

He has been recognised as one of the most influential financial advisers in Britain and was named Best Blogger of the Year by finance journalists at the Media Adviser Awards.

Martin is frequently featured in the press and has seen two of his books named WH Smith Business Book of the Month.

Away from work, Martin is father to three smallish children and is a keen runner, completing this year's London Marathon in 3 hours 39 minutes.

Nick Bamford

Nick is a very experienced Chartered Financial Planner and was the previous Chairman of the Society of Financial Advisers (SOFA).

Nick has been an independent financial adviser since 1989. He has spent his entire working life in the financial services profession.

He is an established Media IFA, appearing on television and radio to discuss personal finance issues.

When not working, Nick enjoys spending time with his grandchildren and watching as much sport on TV as he can!

Andrew Neligan

Andrew is one of an exclusive group of advisers to be a Chartered Financial Planner and Certified Financial Planner (CFP) professional.

He is a graduate of Aston University where he holds an honours degree in Managerial and Administrative Studies. He holds the Advanced Diploma in Financial Planning from the Chartered Insurance Institute.

Outside of work, Andrew is competes in triathlons and tackled his first half-Ironman distance triathlon this summer.

Thank you

This book could not have been written without the kind support of the team at Informed Choice – in particular Andy, Lizanne, Shelley and Emma.

We would also like to thank all of our clients who have provided inspiration for the contents of this book.

Finally, we thank our families, friends and the retail financial services community for its kind support.

Jigsaw School

All proceeds from the sale of this book will go to The Jigsaw Trust.

The Jigsaw Trust is a registered charity (no. 1075464) that aims to improve the lives of those affected by autism through the provision of high quality, accessible, educational, vocational and wellbeing services.

Established in 1999, the Trust was founded by a small group of parents of children diagnosed with autism.

In the same year as the charity was founded, the Trust raised enough funds to set up The Jigsaw CABAS® School.

Informed Choice is a proud supporter of The Jigsaw Trust.

You can find out more at www.jigsawschool.co.uk.

Contents

Introduction

Prepare your plan	9am
Destroy your debt	10am
Terrific tax	11am
Super savings	Midday
Protect your wealth	1pm
Invest to win	2pm
Secure your retirement	3pm
Consider care fees	4pm
Initiate inheritance tax planning	5pm
Assess your advisers	6pm

Your annual wealth check

Introduction

"The best thing about the future is that it comes one day at a time" – Abraham Lincoln

The purpose of this book is to give you a guide that will enable you to take control of your finances (hence the expanded title of the book *Your Money Day - One day to take control of your finances*)

Can you really read a book and achieve such a goal in one day? We believe you can but you will be the ultimate judge of this.

And anyway, why one day? Well we guess that is because if we had a tenner for every time we have heard it said, "I will get round it to it one day" we would be wealthier Financial Planners than we are now!

But seriously, you can put a good financial plan together in a day if you follow the guide we have set out in this book.

It looks at short, medium and long-term aspects of financial planning and sets out the key items you need to consider.

Questions, questions, questions

Your Money Day is also full of questions and (without sounding too pretentious) we absolutely agree with the French philosopher Voltaire who said "You should judge a man by his questions not by his answers" (although we will try to provide some answers as well!)

Each chapter has both a heading and a time. If you really do set aside a day to sort out your finances and take back control then maybe you could use our suggested timing as an agenda.

Taking our advice about what to eat for breakfast, lunch and dinner is of course purely optional!!

The purpose of this book

So what will this book do for you? It, we hope, will make you think.

One of the most valuable things we do for our clients at Informed Choice is to challenge their thinking. We do this in this book by asking you a lot of questions.

We won't be sat in the room with you whilst we are doing this, so it won't come across as some kind of interrogation, but if it helps you can imagine one of the three of us being there with you and tilting our head and gently asking you when you respond to our question "Why do you say that?"

What will you find in this book?

Chapter one is all about **preparing your plan**. We explain the importance of financial planning and how you might go about setting your goals.

Chapter two of the book will look at a subject dear to the heart of Financial Planners world wide - **debt**.

Debt is a drag. Whilst some forms of debt make real sense, borrowing through a mortgage to buy a house for example, long-term debt means that you may fail to achieve some of your other financial planning goals, building a big enough retirement fund to retire early for example.

We look at good debt and bad debt and help you to differentiate between them.

But most importantly in this chapter we encourage you to have a plan to arrive at your 'debt freedom day'; that magic moment in the future when you have cleared all of your outstanding liabilities.

Chapter three looks at **tax**. Not in a boring academic sort of way but in a way that helps you understand that whilst you have to pay all the tax that you are legally required to pay there are tax reliefs and allowances available that will help you to achieve your financial planning objectives.

In chapter four we examine the need for **savings**. Short term savings are a foundation on which to build longer-term financial plans.

Without a doubt having an emergency fund is a key plank of financial security. How much that emergency fund is depends entirely upon you as an individual.

Are you earning the most on your savings accounts that you can? Cash is and always will be King and one key learning point we want to get across is that of never investing cash that you cannot afford to lose or a the very least see fall in value.

Chapter five examines another fundamental of financial planning - making sure that in the event of a long term illness or disability, or even the death or critical illness of a 'breadwinner', that your family remains financially robust.

We are all of course immortal and none of us will ever contract one of the dread diseases but transferring risk through **insurance** at least should always be considered even if ultimately rejected.

In chapter six we start to look at the **investment** of money for the medium to long term.

We set out our six step approach to investing and explain why each of those steps is crucial to getting the best results from your investments.

As grand as it sounds we also set out our investment philosophy and it will be very interesting to see if you agree with our common sense and pragmatic approach to investing.

In chapter seven we look at the big one! There is little doubt in our mind that it is the subject of **pensions** that causes the most difficulty for most normal human beings. A subject beset with archaic and strange language designed to confuse!

We will explain what you need to consider in plain English and give you that much needed track to run on.

We have an ageing population in the UK and many may arrive in later life unable to care for themselves. The cost of **care fees** can be enormous, certainly north of £1,000 per week in the South East of England. It can also be a cost that destroys the prospect of an inheritance for the next generation.

Chapter eight looks at how you can deal with that day when an elderly relative, perhaps mother or father, can no longer look after themselves at home.

In chapter nine we look at **estate planning**. How do you make sure that you can pass on as much of the estate that you have worked so hard to build up to your children or grandchildren. Perhaps most importantly we describe the steps that you can take to mitigate the 40% tax that is Inheritance Tax.

Because personal finances are often complex, we've dedicated chapter ten to the subject of **advice**. We explain how to assess your advisers and what to look for in a good financial adviser, solicitor and accountant.

Most importantly, we look at how these three types of professional adviser can most effectively work together for your benefit.

The final chapter is about the **annual wealth check** we think you should carry out each and every year. This is essential to ensure your plans remain on track, as circumstances and goals often change. Without an annual wealth check you risk going off course and ending up in entirely the wrong destination.

We hope that you find this book both useful and enjoyable. We have certainly enjoyed writing it in one day. It challenged our thinking and we hope it does the same for you.

Remember that all proceeds from the sale of this book go to The Jigsaw Trust; a local registered charity which we are very proud to support.

Martin, Andrew & Nick
20th August 2013

Prepare your plan

"Everyone has a plan 'till they get punched in the mouth" – Mike Tyson

9am

We go to work, either for ourselves or for someone else, get paid each month and spend our money on various items.

Some of those items will be essential (mortgage repayments or rent, utility bills and council tax for example) others will be discretionary (clothing, holidays and entertainment would be good examples) but how many of us have any direction for our finances? A direction that is aligned with what we want to achieve in our lives?

You may love your job or you may hate it but at some point, some day you will reach a stage when you say to yourself, and may be your partner too, that you have had enough.

You no longer wish to go to work anymore, you can no longer bear the commute, or perhaps your colleagues, and you want to stop.

You will arrive at the point where you prefer to spend your days doing what it is you love most in life but have never had the chance to do so.

Maybe you wish to travel the world, may be wish to learn to play an instrument, write a novel, spend more time in the garden or with your loved ones.

The problem will be that you will open up your treasure chest to see how much wealth you have to support your desired lifestyle and there will not be enough. There will not be capital to draw upon or to provide ongoing income payments for life.

There will not be enough because you are going through your working life not giving enough thought to the future and how you may fund your retirement.

Or, it may be that you have given some thought to the future but it has either not been enough or it has been misguided.

You may have been diligently paying off your mortgage each month or making contributions to your company pension but without proper forethought it is likely that, prudent as you have been, there will be a gap between what you need to have to live your life and what you will have.

This is where Financial Planning plays a vital role in your future financial wellbeing.

Multi-stage approach

Financial Planning is a multi-stage approach that allows you to understand whether you are on course to live the lifestyle you wish to and, if you are not, what actions you have to take to make it achievable.

The starting point is to address what it is you wish to achieve in life. Do you know what you want to achieve?

Perhaps you wish to:

- Retire early,

- Repay your mortgage within ten years,

- Have a career change so you can feel more fulfilled,

- Buy a bigger house,

- Buy a holiday home,

- Buy a yacht,

- Take time off and help those less fortunate,

- Ensure financial security for your family,

- Something else

This is an exercise that many people struggle with defining but it does not need to be particularly bold or ambitious; you may not wish to dedicate your life to others or to live like a multi-millionaire.

As mentioned above, you many simply want to retire at a particular age and know you can maintain your existing lifestyle and have no money worries.

Achieving financial independence is not for the wealthy only.

Wealthy people can find achieving their goals as hard, if not harder than, those less wealthy if their lifestyles are more expensive. After all a frugal person requires less capital and income than someone who has more of a flamboyant lifestyle.

Maintaining your lifestyle

In our experience most people want to maintain their lifestyles in retirement.

Not many want to upgrade it and spend far more than they do currently, aside from increasing the amount they spend on holiday, but certainly, without exception, nobody wishes to see their lifestyle downgraded. But this does not mean that it won't happen.

You may have one overriding goal or you may have a number that are linked together.

For example, if you wish to retire at 55 you will probably want to be mortgage free by then too. If you wish to buy a yacht you will probably want to be able to afford not to work so that you can sail it.

Lifetime cash flow forecasting

Once these goals have been established (and evidence suggests that goals that are specific and written down are more likely to be achieved) you can work out if they are achievable based upon your current position.

This is where Lifetime Cash Flow Forecasting comes in.

Put simply, Lifetime Cash Flow Forecasting predicts your future financial position based upon your current position and by making assumptions about the future including future income expectations, asset growth and inflation.

It provides a visual representation of your wealth over time so that you can see if your goals are achievable.

There will be one of three outcomes: you will have too much, you will not have enough or you are nicely on course.

If it looks like you are going to die with too much wealth you may conclude that you don't need to expose your capital to any investment risk or that you can afford to give capital away and avoid paying income tax, inheritance tax or both.

If it appears that your goals are not achievable, that you will not be able to retire when you wish to or that you will not be able to buy a yacht and afford to stop working, you can then decide what actions you need to take to make them achievable.

It may be that you dedicate more of your income now to funding your future or you take more investment risk with your capital to give it the opportunity to grow at a faster rate.

If the forecast suggests that you are on course, great! But it may also allow you to bring forward some of your goals. You may be able to pay off the mortgage sooner or buy the boat earlier.

Another important consideration is to establish what impact a major catastrophe such as death, an accident or the diagnosis or a serious illness will have on the ability for you or your loved ones to live the lifestyle desired.

If you or your partner dies what impact will that have on your ability to repay your mortgage or continue to fund your retirement? Similarly if you were to have an accident or an illness that causes the loss of household income.

By calculating what ramifications a loss of income would have it enables you to put a number on what gaps exist and what the cost would be of plugging these gaps with a life assurance policy.

So Financial Planning becomes the first in a number of important steps that you must take in order to give yourself financial security and financial wellbeing so that whatever matters to you most in life becomes a reality.

The rest of the book examines what actions you can take to ensure your money is working hard enough and efficiently so that your plan becomes a reality.

You will find out how:

- To pay off debt

- To minimise the tax you pay (legally!)

- Be efficient with your savings

- Protect your wealth

- Invest sensibly

- Plan for your retirement

- Consider care fees

- Avoid inheritance tax

- Ensure you are getting value when you seek financial advice.

Destroy your debt

"A man in debt is so far a slave" – Ralph Waldo Emerson

10am

Debt is a drag on your ability to meet your financial goals and objectives.

When talking to clients, they can generally distinguish between 'good' and 'bad' debt.

Most people, at some point in their lives, raise a mortgage to buy property. They tend to plan to use a mortgage to afford this massive purchase.

Most people can appreciate the difference between this sort of debt (mortgages) and the sort of frivolous debt used to fund short-term purchases, on things such as plasma screen TVs or foreign holidays.

In general terms, raising debt to purchase an appreciating asset such as a property, is considered a good use of debt.

Taking on debt to fund an asset which loses value or carries no intrinsic value is typically a bad idea.

What happens next?

Always think ahead – debt might be affordable today but what happens to your household budget when interest rates go up?

Model the future. You can afford debt today. What happens when interest rates go to 2%, 4% or even higher. Is it still affordable?

Thinking specifically about mortgages, it's fine if you can afford a five bedroom house today, but do you actually need it? Is a more affordable property today more suitable for your needs?

Secured or unsecured?

There is a big difference between secured and unsecured debt. Secured debt is linked to an asset, typically a property. It tends to be paid back over a much longer term than unsecured debt, which tends to be short-term in nature.

Secured debt also tends to be cheaper than unsecured debt on a like for like basis, although the total cost of repaying secured debt tends to be higher over the longer term simply because you pay for it for longer and it tends to involve a larger amount borrowed.

Repayment or interest only?

It's harder to obtain an interest only mortgage today than it has been historically, simply because the banks and financial services regulators recognise the risks involved in not having a suitable debt repayment strategy in place.

Interest only as a repayment strategy tends to be better suited to those who prefer to take greater risks, or at least have the capacity to take risks.

It might cost you less each month in terms of your total repayment, as theoretically you have the assistance of investment gains to help you towards your total repayment goal.

With a capital repayment mortgage you know for certain that the mortgage will be fully repaid at the end of the term, assuming you keep up the repayments.

It also means that, as the capital is repaid, the interest cost of servicing the debt reduces, so more of the repayments each month go towards repaying the capital.

Debt can be useful

We are not sure that avoiding debt entirely is a realistic strategy. Debt can be useful, when it is used for the right reasons, with the right plan in place to repay it.

Where debt becomes problematic, and in some cases life inhibiting, is where individuals overstretch and borrow beyond their capacity, or where their circumstances change unexpectedly and they are unable to keep up with debt repayments.

Pay off debt or invest capital?

A common question we get from clients is whether it is better to pay off debt or invest available capital.

A lot of people seem reluctant to pay off debt when interest rates are so low.

It's important to think about the after tax investment return you receive. For a higher rate taxpayer, you need to obtain an investment return 40% or 50% higher than your mortgage interest rate, after investment charges, to make it worthwhile investing the money rather than paying off debt.

There is often a non-financially quantifiable benefit to repaying debt, and finally owning your own home. We often find a sense of relief, freedom and happiness associated with repaying debt in full.

Although it feels great to repay debt, inevitably your kids (and ultimately grandchildren) will be back looking for a handout.

One simple lesson

We asked our Twitter followers what one simple lesson have you learned about debt.

@gogetemfloyd said:

"One lesson in two parts: only take it if you need it, and when you do, pay it off as quickly as you can".

@fairstone_fm said

"the world revolves around debt i.e. mortgages, vehicle finance etc, but you must manage it correctly"

This is often where people go wrong. They take on debt to buy a property or get a new car in their driveway, but they fail to manage that debt properly.

Worse still is taking on debt to fund a certain lifestyle, where this results in living beyond your means.

Sometimes it is too easy to slip into a comfortable situation of keeping up monthly payments, without thinking about the long-term consequences of

It is worth thinking about the benefits of taking on a mortgage and making repayments in order to own a property and have financial security in the future versus paying rent, which only provides longer term value to the landlord!

Many people view rental payments as 'wasted money', as it is money exchanged each month for a place to live, rather than money for a place to live **and** ownership of that property in later life.

You can almost view your mortgage as part of your retirement strategy. The aim should always be to repay this debt by the time you retire. This then results in a significant reduction to your outgoings in addition to the security of somewhere to live in later life.

Buy to let investing

A lot of Financial Planners warn their clients about the perils of buy to let property investing, but we all know people who have done this successfully.

We can think of two clients who we are currently working with who are coming into substantial amounts of money. The message to them has been quite clear; consider residential property to rent out as they already have exposure to other risk assets.

Buy to let investing is not as risky as it often sounds, assuming you understand and appreciate all of the risks involved.

Properties can be expensive to maintain, good tenants can be difficult to find and there is always the risk that the value of the property will go down.

That said, as part of a well diversified and long-term investment plan, buy to let investing is often worth considering.

Questions about debt

Some question to ask yourself about debt:

Do I really need to borrow this money? Can I find it from another source?

For example, if I have money already in savings and investments, would it be better to take this money and use it for this purpose.

Am I a rate tart? Am I just moving my credit card balances around to get access to a better interest rate, rather than following a defined repayment plan?

Should I be seeking expert independent advice on mortgages and debt or can I go it alone?

What plan do I have to repay my debts? Is this plan robust and will it stand the test of time?

Can I change my mortgage provider to get access to lower interest rates, so more of my monthly payments go towards paying off the debt rather than servicing the interest payments.

Pay off expensive debt first

Great tip on Twitter from @edinmortadvice:

"...Pay off the most expensive debt first"

It should not always be the biggest debt that you focus on repaying first, but the most expensive. For most people your mortgage tends to be the lowest cost debt you have, albeit the biggest.

The most expensive debts tend to be things like credit cards, store cards and overdrafts. Find out what interest rate you are paying (the APR) and list these from most to least expensive. Start off by repaying the most expensive first, even it is represents the smallest debt.

Really bad debt

Store cards are usually a bad idea. They are often sold by people with no understanding of debt, tie you in to shopping at one place (so you can't shop around for a better deal) and come with horribly expensive interest rates.

We have seen store cards described as loyalty or discount cards.

Of course assuming you can repay the balance in full each month, there is no real harm in using a store card to take advantage of an immediate discount.

Another Twitter tip

@edinmortadvice also points out that low rates today mean you should overpay each month or shorten your payment date, or face a future payment shock.

This is a very important issue to consider in the current economic environment where we have very low interest rates and the Bank of England effectively preannouncing that interest rates will stay very low until unemployment falls to a target level.

We don't expect to see interest rates go up for a couple of years; maybe until 2015 or even as late as 2017 if the economic recovery is slower than expected.

What people should be doing in these circumstances is taking the money they save each month and repaying debt, rather than spending it.

Of course the government and Bank of England want you to be spending your money on the High Street, as this is what will drive the economic recovery (and is the purpose of low interest rates).

Ideally what you want is for everyone else to go out there and spend their money, while you chip away at your debts and take advantage of low interest rates.

Keep in mind that these low interest rates are not the norm. They might feel normal right now but they are exceptional and they will go up in the future.

Get help...quickly!

If you get into trouble with debt, seek help quickly. There is never any good reason to avoid opening an envelope and addressing your debt problems.

When seeking help, there are plenty of great sources which are free and entirely impartial. A few to consider are Citizens Advice, Consumer Credit Counselling Service and National Debtline.

Be really careful when looking for any of these online, as a Google search can easily lead you to commercial organisations masquerading as charities!

Sort out your debt today

This is the day when you sort out your finances. Here are the issues you should consider and actions you might want to take today.

1 - Do the calculation to find out your own 'debt freedom day'. Set a date in the future when you want to be free of debt and calculate what this means in terms of making overpayments.

2 - When dealing with couples, we often find that one or other will take the lead role when dealing with finances. When there is debt there, particularly when there is any debt problem, sharing the responsibility for debt management and communicating the issues is healthy. Very often your partner will have a different perspective on managing the debt.

In the same way that it's not a good idea to not open the envelope, failing to share with the other person your debt management concerns is a bad idea and simply defers problems to a later date, when they often harder to deal with.

3 - Don't rely on an inheritance from your parents as your mortgage repayment strategy. We look at inheritance tax and care fees later on in this book, but you might find that what you expected to come your way later on does not materialise.

4 - Debt is a part of most people's lives during their lifetime. It is another part of Financial Planning. Having debt is not an exceptional set of circumstances, but you do need to be able to manage it.

In some circumstances, having debt and managing it well is beneficial. It serves to improve your credit record.

We have come across examples of people who have never had a credit card, personal loan or even a mobile phone contract. When they come to wanting a mortgage later, the bank has no way of knowing whether they will manage their repayments responsibly as they have not established any form of track record.

Having some debt and managing it responsibly is no bad thing.

Terrific tax

"The hardest thing to understand in the world is the income tax" – Albert Einstein

11am

Within this chapter we focus on two of the most important types of tax – income tax and capital gains tax.

Other types of tax are available (!), but we believe these two are the most important for investors to understand as they take control of their personal financial planning.

Income tax

You need to make sure that you pay the right amount of income tax.

PAYE codings are often wrong so it is important to check you are paying the right amount each month. It is very easy to either overpay or underpay the right amount of tax each year, which can quickly build up a big credit or debt with the taxman.

It is quite common to pay too much income tax. Back in 2010, it was estimated that 4.3 million people in Britain had paid an average of £419 too much income tax!

This is money that could be better used to meet other financial objectives, so paying the right amount of income tax is very important.

Legitimately avoid income tax

We are quite intrigued by current HMRC views on this subject. They recently came up with the term 'aggressive tax avoidance'. This feels like a politically motivated issue. In this time of austerity, the government would love to abolish all tax reliefs.

Have the following to hand

On Your Money Day, make sure you have the following in front of you:

-your PAYE coding
-a copy of self assessment form you submitted to HRMC
-your P60 and all of your payslips
-if you are self employed, a set of your accounts

Gift Aid

One of the allowances we often see higher rate taxpayers failing to claim is in respect of their charitable donations. Gift Aid is a valuable tax relief.

If you make charitable donations each year via a service such as Just Giving or Virgin Money Giving, it is worth printing off a list of the donations made during the last tax year and providing a copy of this to your accountant so they can claim the difference between the basic and higher rates of tax in your tax return.

Marginal system

A common misconception about income tax is that one rate of tax is applied to all earnings. Income tax is a marginal system, with earnings in different bands charged at different income tax rates.

Another thing to watch out for is different income tax rates on different types of income. Different rates apply to earned income (your salary) and dividend income from shares.

Tough for pensioners

Certain types of income might not have had tax automatically deducted. A good example is state pension income, which is paid gross. It is subject to income tax, assuming your total income exceeds your tax-free personal allowance, but the responsibility for paying tax on it is your own.

We often find that pensioners, who have multiple sources of income in retirement (e.g. state pension, occupational pension and annuity income as well savings interest) find themselves in a complex tax situation because they need to account for all of these payments.

Another misconception we sometimes come across is that children don't pay tax. They do, but often don't earn enough to pay tax as any earnings are well within their tax-free personal allowance.

It's worth watching out for the '£100 rule', which means that if parents gift enough money to their children to generate £100 or more in interest each year, the interest is taxable in the name of the parent.

In other words, you can't use your kids and their unused personal allowance to avoid paying tax!

If you find yourself in the position where you don't earn enough to pay income tax, but you have savings, you can complete form R85 from the HMRC to receive that interest free of tax and save having to reclaim it in the future.

Use your husband (or wife)

One useful tax planning strategy for married couples or those in a civil partnership is to own assets such as savings in the name of the lower earning spouse.

This means that any income from the asset can be included in an unused personal allowance or taxed at the basic rate of income tax, rather than the higher or highest rates.

Age related personal allowance

We often come across scenarios where clients are over age 65 and have the age related personal allowance but lose some or most of it because their income exceeds the cut-off.

There are types of income which are not included within this limit, including withdrawals from Investment Bonds which are tax-deferred capital withdrawals rather than income taxed immediately.

Using an accountant

At what point should someone use an accountant? Definitely when they are self-employed, have multiple sources of income (including rental income from properties), or have complicated tax affairs (such as capital losses or gains).

Those without the time, knowledge or inclination to manage their own tax affairs should consider paying an accountant to prepare their tax returns, as the value of this is immense.

Non-taxable income

There are various sources of non-taxable income. These include disability living allowance, attendance allowance, lump sum bereavement payments, pension credit, free TV licences of the over 75s, winter fuel payments and Christmas bonus, housing benefit, employment and support allowance, certain types of income support, child benefit (although this does become taxable in some circumstances), guardians allowance, maternity allowance, industrial injuries benefit, severe disablement allowance, war widows pension and young persons bridging allowance.

Investments or savings income from Individual Savings Accounts (ISAs) is free of tax. This makes ISAs a valuable tax planning tool and you should consider using your ISA allowance in full each year, if this is affordable, to shelter your assets from income tax.

Where you have a lodger in your home, the first £4,250 of rent each year is free of income tax under the Rent a Room Relief system. This can provide a useful tax free source of additional income if you have a spare room.

Tax credits are also free of income tax. But you should be careful to notify HMRC of any changes to your circumstances which affect the amount of tax credits you receive, as it is easy to build up a sizeable debt when claiming tax credits to which you are not entitled.

Gambling wins are generally free of tax. Any wins from Premium Bonds from National Savings & Investments are also free of tax.

Salary sacrifice

One of our Twitter followers, @abrahamonmoney, suggested salary sacrifice as a good way of reducing the amount of tax you pay.

If you agree with your employer to reduce your salary and have that reduction paid by your employer into a pension plan instead, both you and your employer will save National Insurance contributions.

Your employer might agree to put into the pension plan some of the National Insurance contributions they save, and that overall might be more beneficial than paying a personal pension contribution from your net pay.

It is worth mentioning that salary sacrifice does reduce your income, however, so if you need a certain income level to obtain a mortgage, then this might not be the right strategy for you. Also consider your death in service benefit which can be a multiple of your gross pay, and therefore reduced by the act of salary sacrifice.

Pension tax relief

Tax reliefs are available when you make pension contributions. You can pay money into a pension plan and receive income tax relief.

This works by the basic rate of income tax being added to your pension fund, because you pay the contribution net of basic rate income tax relief. You then can claim any available higher rate tax relief.

Tax-free investing

There are certain types of investments you can make on which you receive income tax relief. These include Venture Capital Trusts (VCTs) and Enterprise Investment Schemes (EISs).

VCTs offer income tax at 30% with a maximum investment of £200,000 a year. For investments made into EISs, the income tax relief is also 30%.

Tax tail, investment dog

When it comes to obtaining any form of tax relief, it is important not to let the 'tax tail wag the investment dog'. Tax relief is a bonus, rather than a reason to do something in its own right.

It is never a good idea to invest money simply to get the tax relief, unless that investment is suitable for you in its own right. Any relief gained may be lost through investment losses.

Capital gains tax

As with income tax, paying capital gains tax is a sign of investment success. If means that the value of your investment assets have grown over and above the annual allowance.

Because all of us receive a capital gains tax annual allowance, investing money to generate a gain rather than an income can often be tax efficient.

You pay capital gains tax when you dispose of certain assets which have grown in value since you acquired them. This means you pay a tax on the gain, rather than a tax on the entire value of the investment.

The first £10,900 of capital gains in each tax year are free of capital gains tax, and this is a valuable allowance often overlooked by those trying to reduce their total tax liability.

CGT free assets

You don't pay any capital gains tax on certain types of assets, including your home, known technically as your principle private residence.

You also don't pay any capital gains tax on investments gains within an ISA or pension. Insurance Bonds from insurance companies are also not subject to any capital gains tax.

Personal assets below the value of £6,000 don't suffer any kind of capital gains tax. These are known as chattels.

You have to be careful that when you sell things that you believe are not subject to capital gains tax, HMRC does not view this as trading income.

What about trustees?

Trustees as well as individuals pay capital gains tax. They have different rates and allowances, but if you are the trustee of a trust then you will be liable for CGT if the trust disposes of assets which make a gain.

Really you should be seeking professional advice to make sure you are not paying more capital gains tax than necessary. Timing can become a factor, so accountancy advice is important.

If you make a loss on a taxable asset, this can be carried forward and offset against a future gain. This is why accountancy advice on capital gains tax is so important, as accountants will know all of the rules and available exemptions.

CGT or IHT?

There is an important trade-off between capital gains tax and inheritance tax. If someone dies and leaves you their assets, there is no CGT payable. But if the investment grows in value before you sell it, it will be subject to capital gains tax from the date of death to the date of disposal.

It is possible transfer assets to a spouse or civil partner to maximise available allowances and also move taxable gains into a lower tax band.

Tax on Your Money Day

What should you do on your money day in respect of tax?

Get a value for all of your savings, investments and other assets. Identify which you pay tax and which are tax-free.

Identify any profits on your investment assets and consider making disposals within your annual allowance, or to take advantage of any capital losses you have carried forward.

To protect as much as possible of your assets from income and capital gains tax, make sure you have used your full ISA allowance, not just the cash ISA allowance.

Consider transferring assets to the lower earning spouse or civil partner to take advantage of their unused personal allowance or lower tax rates.

To take advantage of your available capital gains tax allowance, you might consider funding your ISA each year by selling taxable investments.

Speak to your employer to arrange salary sacrifice pension contributions.

Check you are paying the right amount of income tax! Is your tax coding correct.

Celebrate any capital gains tax due, because it means you have made a profit on your investments!

Super savings

"Number one, cash is king..." – Jack Welch

Midday

In all of our years of experience, we have never witnessed a significant problem for someone who claims to have too much money held in cash.

Everyone needs savings. Savings provide a safety net for emergencies.

Your emergency fund

Like all good Financial Planners, we recommend that people hold an emergency fund, in cash, equivalent to three to six months of typical expenditure.

When things go wrong financially, you can call on this emergency fund to keep you out of real trouble, such as being unable to keep up mortgage repayments or getting into debt.

Discipline is important here and you should save a certain amount of money each month. You soon get used to the money not being available to spend when you have been allocating it automatically to savings instead.

Saving is better than buying

If you save to purchase a discretionary/luxury item, once you get to the point you can afford it you are more likely to question whether you really need it, as you have experienced the sacrifice of saving the money instead of spending it.

Saving to buy something you really want also makes it cheaper in the long run as you don't have the cost of servicing the debt to contend with.

Shop around

One of the challenges many of our clients are faced with is getting the best return on their cash savings.

Maintaining the best return is also challenging, as the most competitive interest rates tend to fluctuate wildly.

It is essential to shop around. There is huge difference between the most and least competitive interest rates.

Savers tend to be frustrated right now with the very low interest rates on offer, but actually they are more realistic rates than when Icelandic banks were offering unsustainable rates in excess of 6%. Interest rates tend to reflect the reality of risk versus reward.

Save more or repay the mortgage?

A good question from @Ian_Cooper on Twitter, asking whether it is worth saving anything (other than an emergency fund) before paying off a mortgage.

In an ideal world you would want to do both; pay off your mortgage and build savings assets at the same time. We are a big fan of mortgage repayment.

You should work out what your priorities are and then identify the opportunity cost of each option. It tends to be the case that there is a much stronger financial argument for repaying your mortgage rather than saving money.

The after tax and inflation return on your savings would need be higher than the interest rate on your mortgage to make saving a better option from a purely financial perspective.

However, diverting all of your available income to repay your mortgage can leave you with no liquidity later in life and also no capital from which to generate an income.

The question that is often asked is whether it is better to take advantage of a fixed interest rate or a variable rate. This all depends on the difference between the two rates and also your expectation of future interest rates.

Even if you do decide to fix for one year, generally you can get hold of your money but you lose out on higher interest available.

How safe is your cash?

During the global financial crisis, interestingly it wasn't the falling value of investment markets that bothered many of our clients but concerns around the safety of their savings account.

How safe if your money? There is always institutional risk behind keeping money in the bank, as we saw in the bankruptcy of some banks during the global financial crisis.

In the UK, savers are well protected by the Financial Services Compensation Scheme (FSCS) which guarantees deposits up to £85,000 a year per licensed deposit taker per individual.

So if instead you have a joint account, you both would receive protection from the FSCS of up to £170,000. FSCS protection on deposit accounts takes into account any debts you also have with that institution, so it might be worth keeping your savings and mortgage with different banks!

NS&I protection

Another place where your savings are well protected is National Savings & Investments because these are backed by HM Treasury.

So if you have significant amounts of savings and you don't want to separate them between different banks to take advantage of the FSCS protection, using NS&I could be an option to consider.

However, you do tend to get much lower interest rates from NS&I by virtue of the financial security they offer.

Consider a cash ISA

For the first £5,760 of your savings, you might consider a cash ISA, simply to avoid paying tax on the interest you earn.

Some gross interest ISA accounts actually pay you less than the net interest on ordinary savings accounts, so take care to shop around and get the best deal.

Whilst we would never recommend that you base your financial planning around the prospect of winning a prize, you should buy a few Premium Bonds because with the top prize of £1m, you never know, you might just get lucky!

Rule of 72

One drawback of keeping money in cash savings is that price inflation erodes the buying power of your money over time. Therefore if inflation rates exceed interest rate, as we are currently experiencing, you automatically see the purchasing power of your money fall. Particularly as you could be paying income tax on your savings as well.

The rule of 72 applies here. By dividing the rate of inflation by 72, you can see how long it takes for the buying power of your money to halve. For example, if price inflation was 3% a year, your savings would halve in value in real terms in 24 years.

Peer-to-peer

Away from conventional savings with banks or building societies, one market which is developing is peer-to-peer lending. The Internet makes this easier to facilitate, with the ability to effectively lend your money to a group of individuals with a certain credit rating, often in return for a much higher rate of interest than you can achieve on the High Street.

There is also a social benefit, as those who might not be able to get access to capital at an affordable rate can access the savings market. Anything to avoid the extortionate rates charged by payday lenders!

If you are thinking of lending some of your money to a member of your family, make sure you document it properly to avoid getting into a disagreement at a later date.

Agree the terms of the loan including when you expect it to be repaid and how much interest will be paid. Many will prefer to keep their savings with an established and regulated organisation such as a bank.

Where do you find the money to save?

If your household budget suggests that you already spend your income in full each month, how do you find the money to save?

A good start is to list all of your expenditure and then prioritise this spending in relation to your financial objectives. Deciding whether you would rather have financial freedom in twenty years' time or an expensive satellite TV package today (long term financial satisfaction or short term gratification) can make this decision easier to make.

For example, the cost of 20 cigarettes a day over the course of 20 years is £58,254. This is of course ignoring any contribution from compound interest rates or investments returns, and also ignoring future tax rises.

It also ignores the cost savings you will achieve as a non-smoker on various insurances during your lifetime. Smoking makes no financial sense whatsoever (except when it comes to purchasing an annuity in later life).

Looking at it another way, if you spend £1,000 on a TV today, instead you could earn 5% a year for 20 years it would be worth £2,653.

Savings on Your Money Day

What should you do in respect of your savings on your money day?

Check the interest rate you are receiving on your savings. Could you improve this elsewhere by shopping around?

Calculate what three to six months committed expenditure represents and then set this as a target for your emergency fund.

If you already have savings in excess of your emergency fund target level, consider whether you might be better off repaying any debt you have.

Have you utilised your cash ISA allowance for the current tax year? Consider sheltering some of your interest from income tax.

Does the total value of your savings exceed the FSCS protection limit of £85,000 per individual per bank?

Would it better to have savings in your partner's name rather than your own, if he or she is a basic rate or non-taxpayer?

Review your expenditure. Can you make savings that can be better used elsewhere; switching energy provider, for example?

Protect your wealth

"I just don't think there's a suncream that gives you enough protection" – Brooke Burke

1pm

Many of the conversations we have with our clients revolve around the importance of them ensuring financial security for themselves and their loved ones.

As recently as 2011, a survey by Scottish Widows found that 56% of adults in the UK did not have any life assurance in place to secure their family income.

There are some circumstances where life assurance might not be necessary. If you are single with no financial dependents and no debts, life assurance might not be high on your list of financial priorities.

These are not just considerations for when a catastrophe has occurred but for when you are fit and healthy. This is the time to be thinking carefully about protection and putting in place the relevant measures to ensure the financial security for your family.

Thinking about death

When we think about financial protection, we often think about death. Life assurance is sometimes a tricky topic as nobody really wants to think about dying. However, as it is inevitable, it is something we must all consider.

How much income or capital would your family need in the event of your death?

This is often a question answered by thinking about the need to repay any debts and then maintain a certain standard of living.

We don't think we have ever come across someone who has too much life assurance cover.

The decision to put in place life assurance is often an extension of your attitude towards risk. Some people prefer to use those resources they already have in place to 'self-insure' against the risk of death and this is a healthy approach to financial planning.

However, it can take time to build up sufficient capital.

Income or capital?

Will your family need income or capital when you die? Capital is often necessary to repay capital debts, such as mortgages. To maintain a lifestyle, income is often a more appropriate benefit to receive.

If you have capital for this purpose, difficult decisions need to be made in order to invest the money to generate an income.

If you buy life in the form of a capital sum assured, you can then use that capital to invest for income for your family. If there is any left over, that capital can flow down a generation.

An income on death

The capital sum assured route might be more expensive than buying a life assurance policy which pays out a series of income payments, also known as Family Income Benefit.

Family Income Benefit also means you don't have to worry about managing the money to generate an income.

The need for life assurance often changes during your lifetime. Perhaps you need a certain amount of life assurance in place until your children finish school or University.

Our clients often establish life assurance with a term to coincide with the full repayment of their mortgage.

By calculating the amount of capital you would need to generate a certain level of income you can readily contrast the costs of buying term assurance, which pays a capital sum on death, with Family Income Benefit, which pays an income on death for the remainder of the policy term.

A reasonable yield on capital to generate income for your family might be 3%. You can use this figure to consider the capital amount you would need on death to generate a certain level of income payment.

A question of trust

There is also the question of whether you place a life assurance policy in trust.

From an inheritance tax and speed of payment point of view, this is important. Trusts are about getting the right money in the right hands at the right time.

If the life assurance is to repay debt, the use of a trust may be less important, but a simple and inexpensive trust can still make sense in these circumstances.

We often find that life assurance policies have been established and are not in trust, so aggravate the inheritance tax position of the estate.

What about existing benefits?

Also think about any existing benefits you have from employment or the value of any pensions which would provide a benefit on death. Savings and investments are often an overlooked source of benefits of death.

Life assurance is surprisingly good value to put in place, particularly if you are younger and a healthy non-smoker.

For a 35 year old non-smoking male it would cost £60.57 per month for a sum assured of £1.2m over a term of 20 years.

Critical illnesses

As well as death, you should think about what would happen if you contracted a critical illness.

Critical illness cover tends to be a lot more expensive than life assurance cover, as the likelihood of contracting a critical illness is that much greater.

For example, the 35 year old non-smoking male in the example above would pay £330.40 per month for £1.2m of critical illness cover over a 20 year term for standard rates currently available.

This difference in premiums suggests that he is around six times more likely to contract a critical illness than to die before age 55.

Quality of cover is paramount when considering critical illness cover, so price tends to be a lesser consideration. Check carefully to see which conditions are covered and don't make assumptions about coverage for certain critical illnesses.

That said, the Association of British Insurers (ABI) standards for critical illness cover are now fairly robust and cover most of the conditions people would expect to see included.

However, be aware that the underwriting of critical illness cover is particularly robust and items such as family history will be closely examined by the underwriter.

Decreasing term assurance

If you have a capital repayment mortgage and want to put in place life assurance cover to repay this on your death, you might consider decreasing term assurance (sometimes called mortgage protection).

This type of life assurance cover reduces in value each year in line with the outstanding value of your mortgage. Decreasing term assurance therefore tends to represent better value than level term assurance, as the potential sum assured becomes lower over time.

Non-disclosure

There have been many examples of life assurance claims which are rejected or reduced due to non-disclosure.

It is essential to fully disclose to the insurer all material facts which might influence their decision about the application. We also suggest keeping a copy of your application, as a reminder of what you have told them.

Protecting your income

Another important type of protection to consider is income protection insurance.

In the event that you are off work due to sickness or disability for a long period of time, you may want to ensure that your family continues to receive a regular income.

This also saves you from having to rely on the State for support or spend your savings to maintain a certain lifestyle.

The cost of this cover depends on a number of factors, including your age, type of occupation, the level of the income benefit, and also how soon after you become ill the payments start (the deferred period). The sooner the payout, the more expensive the cover.

For a 35 year old non-smoking male, Income Replacement Insurance over a term of 20 years offering a benefit of £36,000 a year would cost £15.79 per month. This assumes standard rates currently on offer.

Under current rules, benefits from income replacement insurance are tax-free.

If your employer already provides this type of cover, as some do, you may not need to take out an individual cover. In the event of a valid claim, you would receive the benefit through your payslip.

Note that income protection is entirely different to payment protection which was mis-sold to millions of banking customers!

Private medical insurance

After life assurance, critical illness cover and income protection insurance, you might want to consider private medical insurance.

This is particularly important for the self-employed who may not want to wait around for the NHS to provide treatment.

It is the interaction between the NHS and private medical insurance which works particularly well. The NHS remains spectacular when it comes to dealing with emergencies. But for anything chronic, it makes sense to buy the service privately rather than be subjected to waiting lists.

Get advice

Private medical insurance is something which requires specialist advice. In fact, we suggest independent financial advice in respect of all types of protection, as the consequences of getting it wrong are so severe.

You might use various online supermarkets to shop around and get an idea of the cost of different types of cover, but when it comes to actually putting in place life assurance or income replacement insurance, always use an adviser.

If you are going to buy any type of financial protection, you would be well advised to give up smoking a year or two earlier, as the savings would be significant.

Prioritise

How do you prioritise what type of financial protection you need?

The younger you are, the greater the chances of being off work sick or disabled rather than dying. This means that life assurance tends to be a greater priority later in life.

You need to base the decision to prioritise one type of cover over another on your personal circumstances. There tends to be a sensible blend of income protection insurance and life assurance to provide the family security you need.

In some circumstances, an income protection policy might pay out when a critical illness policy does not, and vice versa. In some circumstances, both would pay out.

The subjectivity of this answer is why you need advice. Sit down with a professional adviser and discuss the actual risks requiring cover in each area, rather than the perceived risks which are dictating your thinking.

Protection on Your Money Day

What do you need to do in respect of protection on your money day?

Start by looking at what protection policies or other benefits you already have in place. This includes looking at what your employer is offering.

Consider what capital and income your family would need in the event of your death. This helps to calculate your protection gap; the gap between the cover you have and cover you need.

Also think about the risks other than dying, which include being unable to work or having a chronic illness requiring private medical care.

In addition to financial protection, we recommend people consider creating what we call a 'death box'.

This should include a copy of your Will, life assurance schedules and contact details for your financial adviser. As grim and morbid as this might sound, it is also very practical and will reduce the amount of hardship faced by your family in the event of your death.

Invest to win

"My philosophy is that if I have any money I invest it in ventures and not have it sitting around" – Richard Branson

2pm

Before you ever invest any money, make sure that you set yourself financial goals and objectives. Investing money because you want 'growth' or 'income' is too imprecise.

Consider what level of growth you need, rather than want, and over what timeframe.

Investing without goals

That said, is there really any harm in investing money without a clear goal?

It certainly makes it harder to determine whether your investments have been successful or not. You also stand a good chance of taking more risk than necessary with your money.

But how do you establish financial goals in the first place before you invest? It is important to ask some searching questions and determine answers to all of the big financial questions.

Searching questions

These include thinking about when you want to retire, how much you will need to fund the lifestyle you want, how much is enough to last for the rest of your life, having enough to pay off any debts including your mortgage, and making sure you can provide what it is you want to provide for future generations.

Once established, your financial goals can drive your investment decisions and you gain a much better understanding of your attitude towards investment risk and indeed your capacity to withstand any investment losses.

Risk

Once you have established financial goals, the next step is to consider how much risk you need to take with your money. You can quickly identify whether there is a mismatch between your risk profile and how much risk you need to take with your money.

How do you determine how much risk you are prepared to take? First, you have to understand what risk is.

Risk is different things to different people. Most of us tend to think about capital risk when considering investments, which means the risk of our money falling in value or us losing money.

Risk to most investors is more about actually losing money than the fall in value itself.

Most people appreciate that volatility is going to happen; the rise and fall in value of the investments. To some extent, within boundaries, this is acceptable but the fear of loss is greater.

Volatility sometimes panics an investor into taking action they do not need to take, such as cashing in an investment and crystallising a loss.

We also often hear peopleblaming products for poor returns, when the focus should be on the underlying investment. Products aren't investments; it is the underlying funds which matter in terms of investment returns.

Institutional risk is also important to consider. This is the risk of an institution, such as a bank, going bust and wiping out the value of investments.

Because you want to sleep soundly at night, it makes sense to invest with institutions which are well established and financially strong.

Other risks

Inflation risk is something we have already covered in the earlier chapter about savings, but is also relevant to investments.

If you are dependent on investments for an income and that income goes down, this income risk is often serious for investors.

When income levels fall, this has an immediate impact on lifestyles, whereas capital values falling can often recover without it being immediately felt.

Asset classes

There are several different types of investment assets to consider. The main ones are cash, fixed interest securities, equities and property.

Cash has already been covered earlier in this book. In addition to savings, it can play an important role within an investment portfolio.

Cash allows other money to remain invested when withdrawals are required. It also allows investors to buy funds at opportune times, and the liquidity is important for covering charges.

Fixed interest securities are effectively the act of lending your money to a government or corporation. In return, they provide a fixed rate of interest and promise to repay your loan at some point in the future.

Examples include corporate bonds issued by companies or government bonds (gilts). These are not without risk as there can be a default on the interest payments, the repayment of capital or both.

However, they are deemed to be lower risk than shares because they are, usually, less volatile and investors may receive some capital back on insolvency.

Equities or shares are about ownership in a company in the hope that the company makes profit and distributes some of that profit in the form of a dividend. There is also the hope that the share price of the company rises in value over time.

Property in the context of investment tends to be commercial property, which might produce rental income and the prospect of capital growth.

Different investment asset classes rise and fall in value at different rates depending on market sentiment and economic cycles.

Risk and reward

Risk and reward is an important concept to understand when investing. The greater the degree of risk you take, the greater the potential for reward. Conversely, the lower the risks you take, the lower the potential for reward.

This relationship between risk and reward is inescapable, so investments offering the prospect of high rewards always come with a high degree of risk.

Your requirement for risk within an investment portfolio will often depend on your age and the term of your investments.
Those approaching retirement might regret holding too many shares in their portfolio, while someone in their twenties just starting out would consider a high allocation in shares more appropriate for their long term growth prospects.

Methods of investing

Once you have established your financial goals and risk profile, and understood the various investment asset classes, the next step is considering the different methods of investing.

The majority of investors should buy collective investment funds, as they are then paying for professional fund management rather than attempting to do this for themselves.

There is a choice to be made between active and passive fund management, with the former offering the opportunity to beat the market, although of course there are no guarantees this will happen.

Passive funds attempt to track a market or investment index, such as the FTSE 100, often at a lower cost than active funds.

Once you have made these decisions, you can think about the shape of your investment portfolio. How much do you need to allocate to each investment asset class and which style of investment management will you use to meet your financial goals.

Six easy investment mistakes to make

1 - Chasing past performance. Never pick investment funds based solely on how well they have done in the past, as they are not guaranteed to be repeated.
2 - Putting all of your money into one single asset class. For example, allocating all of your money to gold is a very high risk strategy.

3 - Believing the hype. When everyone is talking about a particular investment, this is often the sign of an investment 'bubble' rather than a good reason to invest. This mistake can also cover believing claims about funds which offer high growth with low risks.

4 - Crystallising a loss. When investments have fallen in value, this is often the worst time to sell your holdings and being panicked into a decision.

5 - Being wedded to a particular investment style. It is important to be open-minded when it comes to different investment styles, as different styles work best in different circumstances.

6 - Taking 'gin and tonic advice'. Accept that most amateurs do not consistently know better than the professionals. Taking investment advice from your mate down the golf club is often a very bad idea.

Cost of investing

What should you expect to pay in order to invest your money? What does good value for money look like?

There are typically three parties to the investment – the product provider, the fund manager and the adviser.

You should not pay any initial charges to a product provider for investing money. This is so old fashioned and not necessary. These days, the product provider is typically an online wrap provider and you would expect to pay a percentage of the assets you hold with them, typically 0.25%.

The fund manager who takes responsibility for actually managing the investment again should not levy an initial charge in this modern world. You might expect to pay 0.3% of your investment for a passive fund or 0.75% for an actively managed fund.

Finally, your adviser might charge you something to establish the investment portfolio and for the advice they provide. They might also charge an ongoing fee equivalent to 0.5% to 1% of your investment portfolio for providing an ongoing review of your investments and financial plans.

Review your portfolio

When you are investing in stock markets, the value of your money can rise and fall rapidly over a day, week, month or year. Whilst this is no concern if you are investing for the right reasons and taking the appropriate degree of risk, it is important that the manner in which you invest remains appropriate to your goals.

We recommend a comprehensive review of an investment portfolio typically on an annual basis to make sure the underlying asset allocation remains suitable to achieve your goals and the funds you previously selected remain the most appropriate for you.

An investment philosophy

Before investing, it is important to have an investment philosophy. These are the things you believe and apply to your investment decisions.

Here is our own investment philosophy which you might want to use as a framework for creating your own:

As a firm of Chartered Financial Planners, we firmly believe that:

1. Investment success comes from the consistent application of a robust process.

2. Diversification using mainstream asset classes can reduce risk without destroying returns.

3. The bulk of long-term returns come from an asset allocation strategy.

4. It is possible to add extra value through tactical asset allocation decisions and fund selection.

5. Investment decisions should relate to financial planning objectives.

6. Trying to time the market is a strategy doomed for failure.

7. The 'best' funds display consistent risk-adjusted returns combined with low charges.

8. There might be surprises just around the corner, but history informs the most likely long-term outcome.

9. Active management and passive strategies can both play a valuable role.

10. Investors should know and understand the reasons for investing in every part of their portfolio.

Picking suitable funds

Selecting the most suitable investment funds can often be difficult. Without using past performance as a way to determine whether a particular fund is suitable, what other factors should you consider?

Academic research tells us that it is simply not possible to consistently select the 'best' investment funds or identify 'star' fund managers. Our own research process aims to find investment funds that are most likely to deliver consistent performance.

We start with the entire universe of collective investment funds. These are divided into the relevant IMA sectors before we apply our research criteria to each and every fund.

Funds that demonstrate consistent and risk managed returns combined with a low total expense ratio are typically preferred by this research process. We believe that these are three factors which investors should be looking for.

In addition to this formal research process, we are fortunate to have regular contact with all of the leading fund management groups and their managers.

Most investors will not be in a position to interrogate individual fund managers about their approaches, but they can glean a great deal of information from articles and interviews published about the managers.

Investment decisions on Your Money Day

On your money day you should take the following steps in respect of your investments.

Get your investment valuations together and begin the analytical process of understanding what you actually have in place.

It's your money and you should know how it is invested, what mandates you have given people and how it is being managed.

Reconsider your attitude towards investment risk and have a formal assessment of your risk profile.

Consider whether your financial goals have changed over time and what this means for how your investment portfolio is positioned.

Discuss your investment portfolio with your spouse and get their views. We often come across couples where the investment decisions are being driven by one partner rather than both.

If you were starting to invest again, what would you do differently?

We all arrive with portfolio positions that have been created over time and might not reflect the best current practice.

Look at how much you are paying for your investments and whether you are getting good value from each party; the product provider, the fund manager and your adviser.

Secure your retirement

"I'm a little young for retirement" – Joni Mitchell

3pm

The biggest issue for most people is the need to build a sufficiently robust retirement fund. This is because a key financial planning objective is to be able to retire when you want to rather than when the State or indeed your employer tells you that you have to.

We have absolutely moved away from the old way of thinking that men retire at age 65 and women retire at age 60. So the first question to ask yourself is, "When do I want to retire?"

This is not to suggest that you don't enjoy what it is you are doing but perhaps you want to spend more time doing other things that interest you, hobbies for example or simply spending more time with your grandchildren.

Or it could be that you don't enjoy doing what you are doing, you may be stressed out or perhaps tired of work.

Expenditure analysis

The second question you need to ask yourself is "How much retirement income do I need?"

A good way of looking at this is to carry out an expenditure analysis. How much do you spend on things now and how much do you intend or expect to spend on things post retirement?

This can be a really challenging exercise but in our experience it is an important step towards understanding how close you are to being able to retire. This is about carrying out an audit of where you currently are.

What do you already have?

So you know when you want to retire and you know how much retirement income that you need. The next step is to establish how much retirement income you have already accumulated.

You may need to get a projection from your pension provider. This will project using certain contribution and investment growth rates, and future expected interest rates, the level of income that you might expect to get.

In addition you might want to find out how much you will ultimately receive from the State pension system.

Note however that it might well be that your State pension age is later (typically age 66, say) than the age at which you have determined you wish to retire.

You can apply for a forecast at www.direct.gov. Be aware though that the Government pension system is a bit of a 'moving feast' and what is projected today may be subject to change based on the current revamp of the State pension entitlement.

Other resources

Once you have an estimate of what your private, occupational and State pension benefits might be you need then to consider what other resources you might have at retirement that will also produce retirement income.

A good way to look at this is just because it doesn't have either of the words "pension" or "retirement" on the label it doesn't mean that your savings and investments don't form part of your retirement planning.

So if you have ISAs, a share portfolio or a buy to let property, you might want to establish how much income those assets can produce.

Assume a yield

Use a realistic 'yield' to calculate the income available from your capital.

We think that currently a yield of 3% is quite reasonable providing a sustainable income level and the prospect of some possible capital growth.

Add all these figures up. How much income might all these different assets produce?

Now as an example, imagine that your answer to the question above about how much retirement income you need was £30,000.

Imagine that the audit you have just carried out demonstrated that you might reasonably produce an income of £19,000 from all sources. You have now identified the gap that needs to be filled.

We accept that if the gap of £11,000 needs to be filled over a 20 year period that is a more realistic prospect than if you have to fill the gap over two years.

But this exercise will also inform you about the reasonableness or otherwise of your desired early retirement and we suggest it will lead to these possible outcomes;

- Retirement is going to be a real struggle and you are going to have to continue working for much longer than you actually want to; or

- You may have to scale down your ambitions by living on a smaller retirement income (in which case you may not be able to do all the things you want to or have the lifestyle that you want); or

- You can achieve the retirement age you want and the lifestyle that you want but it requires future financial commitment to do so.

The beauty of this approach is that it introduces some realism into the planning.

You will not be indulging in any "self- kidology" pretending that all is well with your retirement planning when in fact it isn't.

Important steps

The next steps have to some extent been covered in previous chapters but let's refocus on them here.

How is your pension fund invested? Are you taking too much risk or possibly too little risk with your retirement plans?

Revisit the chapter about investing and consider how you might apply some of the investment advice we have provided there to your retirement funds.

Work out how much extra you need to save to get sufficient capital together to produce the income gap that you need to fill.

Remember this is not just about saving in a conventional pension plan; you may want to consider all the possible alternatives such as ISAs, share portfolios and even property.

Of course pension plans have some attractive tax reliefs associated with them but again, as we said in an earlier chapter, you should not let the tax tail wag the investment dog!

There may also be some other options available to you. What may sound radical, but we have seen it work well in practice, and that is the possibility of downsizing your home and buying a smaller retirement property.

The equity that is released from such an exercise can then be invested to generate extra income.

It also follows that it might be cheaper to live in a smaller house (although in practice this may not always be the case)

At retirement options

There are a number of ways in which a conventional pension plan can be converted into income.

This is an area where a lot of people choose to seek truly impartial independent advice because the choices and options are potentially quite complex and in certain cases once the option is chosen it is pretty much fixed.

At retirement, you have a number of choices:

Defer your retirement. This may or may not be acceptable to you. If you have to defer your retirement how long will that be for?

It is interesting to note that retirement doesn't have to be about coming to a complete halt. It might be about working less or doing something different or of a vocational nature.

It could be that retirement is about restructuring your work life balance rather than coming to a full stop.

Purchase a conventional annuity. The most usual way of doing this is to use the fund to purchase a conventional annuity. However annuity rates are pretty dire at the present time and once you have purchased and annuity you are stuck with it.

David Ferguson CEO of the wrap provider Nucleus made a telling comment: *"The market (for annuities) doesn't seem to have evolved remotely in line with changing lifestyles. Annuities feel very 1970s"*

Purchase an investment linked annuity. This provides an income which may change over time depending upon investment returns achieved.

It is not without risk because of course the value of the annuity income might fall as well as rise, so it is by no means suitable for everyone.

Start an income drawdown arrangement. This is also known as an unsecured pension arrangement. Unsecured because rather than purchasing an annuity the pension fund continues to be invested and income is drawn from it.

You will see immediately that this brings both risk and cost to bear and again is not suitable for everyone.

Phase the purchase of your benefits over time. This can work very well and fits nicely with the semi deferral of retirement. Perhaps you work less and earn less but the gap is filled by taking some of your pension plan benefits

Purchase a 'Third Way' Annuity. Put bluntly and somewhat over simplistically these are sort of half-way houses between annuity purchase and income drawdown.

Whilst a detailed analysis of these choices and options is beyond the scope of this book we should point out that there are both advantages and disadvantages to each approach.

Tax free cash lump sum

Typically this amounts to 25% of the value of the pension plan at retirement. It is a much loved benefit and usually it is taken by the plan holder.

But do consider that this is not automatically the best thing to do.

Assuming you have no capital projects in mind or don't intend to spend the money or give it away, then typically it will have to be reinvested to generate further income.

If that is the case then remember that the capital and the income that it generates can both fall in value in the future. It will also require management and the associated costs that go with it.

That said, post retirement it can be quite difficult to generate further capital sums and so this payment could be seen as a one off opportunity.

Questions to answer on Your Money Day

- When do you want to retire?

- How much income will you need in retirement to enjoy the lifestyle that you want?

- Taking into account all your existing pension plans, State benefits and income that might realistically be generated by other savings and investment assets, how much might you get at your desired retirement age?

- By how much income will that fall short of your desired income level?

- How much do you need to commit now and into the future to fill the gap between what you want and how much you currently might receive?

Consider care fees

"Love begins by taking care of the closest ones – the ones at home" – Mother Teresa

4pm

We are all getting older. With advances in medical science comes improved longevity and the increased likelihood that we will need care at some point in our lives.

This means we need to make sure we have the capital and income to provide for a much longer timeframe, well past retirement and to pay for specific care needs.

Retirement lasts longer

Retirement used to be for 15 years or so. Now it is likely to be double that. As a result of living for longer, many are suffering from physical and mental degradation which has an impact on our ability to look after ourselves.

Consequently, the need for care is growing. This places a burden on the financial resources of the individual but also those of the next generation who are, by choice or necessity, required to look after elderly parents or grandparents.

The substantial cost of care fees and their erosion of capital assets mean lower expectations for inheritance in the future.

High cost

The cost of care is very high, on average around £650 a week in the UK. We are conscious that in Surrey, where the authors live and work, typical fees are in the region of £1,000 a week.

In many cases these elderly people are being looked after by their families. However social changes and busy working lives mean this is not always possible.

Our Twitter follower @gregkingston also pointed out there is an emotional and financial drain on a healthy spouse and family.

So what can you do about it?

Paying for care

There is currently no market in the UK for pre-funding the cost of long term care.

Traditional savings and investment products can therefore be used as the vehicle for building up assets to pay for care, as well as equity stored in the value of your home.

It is common for most people to either sell their home or downsize (if there is a healthy spouse who would continue to live in the property) in order to provide capital or income to pay for care.

The government does provide a safety net where individuals have assets below £23,250, although this might not be particularly helpful as it removes the choice of care provider.

Future care cap

Proposals being implemented aim to significantly increase this assets threshold and put a lifetime cap on the cost of some aspects of care. In the meantime, it is usually the responsibility of the individual and their family to cover this expenditure.

Meeting shortfalls

If the cost of care cannot be covered through existing income alone, any shortfall can be met in one of three ways.

Firstly, you may prefer to have the assurance of capital protection and simply drawdown the amounts required from cash savings.

If however the cost of care exceeds the amount of savings, over time they will be completely eroded and therefore investing for capital growth and income maybe the more preferable route. This is of course not without risk.

Investing to generate income and the prospect for capital growth is the second option people will consider when funding the cost of care.

It is worth referring back to the steps you would follow when building an investment portfolio, when considering this option.

Setting a clear financial goal and deciding on an appropriate attitude towards investment risk is important, before constructing a portfolio and selecting suitable funds. In our experience, individuals have a much lower tolerance to investment risk in later life.

The third option is to purchase a care fees annuity which involves the exchange of a capital payment in return for a tax-free guaranteed income for life.

The income payments are tax-free where they are paid directly to the care home for the provision of care services.

The cost of the care fees annuity will depend on the life expectancy of the annuitant and the level of income required, other features attached to the annuity such as inflation and capital protection.

A combination of these three options may also prove to be a satisfactory outcome.

Conflicting objectives

Planning for the cost of care typically involves the person who is responsible for the individual receiving care and the adviser examining all of the relevant options for that individual.

We usually provide advice to the children of the individuals requiring care, often in their capacity as attorney, and these two roles can sometimes bring about conflicting objectives.

Firstly, to ensure that their parent or parents have their care needs adequately provided, and secondly to ensure they have capital passed to them in the form of an inheritance.

Real care must be taken to ensure the children do not fall foul of their duties as attorneys to ensure the individuals' needs are met in full.

Making a decision on the best approach to take often causes a dilemma which can lead to emotional stresses. Your expectation of your mother or father's life expectancy plays a big role.

The lower risk approach is to purchase a care fees annuity, although this can represent poor value should death occur soon after you enter a care home.

Keeping money in savings or investments might be considered a better approach should your expectations of life expectancy be quite short.

Expensive gamble

With the average life expectancy of those in a residential care home at only two years, spending capital to purchase a care fees annuity can feel like an expensive gamble.

It does however act as good insurance against the person needing care living for much longer than expected.

Buying a care fees annuity also serves to ring fence all of the other assets. Regardless of how long the person needing care lives and continues paying care fees, the remaining value of the estate will be secure and not called upon for the purpose of paying these fees.

Care fees inflation

It is worth noting that the rate of care fees inflation is typically higher than the official price inflation figures, so it is important to factor this in to any long term projections.

Care fees planning on Your Money Day

What should you be thinking about on your money day in respect of care fees?

Sit down with elderly parents and have a frank discussion about their future care needs, as well as how these would be paid for.

Get a Lasting Power of Attorney in place. These don't need to be registered until mental capacity is lost, but having them drawn up early makes a great deal of sense as it avoids the costly and time consuming process of applying for guardianship from the Court of Protection.

Work with your parents to understand their income and assets, as well as their preferences for care. Some people are comfortable with residential care while others will want to remain in their own homes for as long as possible, with care brought in.

At the point where an elderly parent needs care, seek professional independent financial advice and carefully consider all of the options.

Initiate inheritance tax planning

"The finest inheritance you can give to a child is to allow it to make its own way, completely on its own feet" – Isadora Duncan

5pm

When it comes to inheritance tax, the clients we work with tend to fall into one of two distinct camps.

They are absolutely furious about the prospect of handing over a substantial part of their estate to the government in the form of inheritance tax.

Alternatively, they take the view that their children or grandchildren are going to inherit far more than they ever did and therefore they are unconcerned about the prospect of an inheritance tax bill of 40% of their taxable estate.

After all, you only pay inheritance tax once you are dead, and if you are not around to see the consequences perhaps it makes you a little immune from its impact.

When we talk to people in the first group, we often find that when the cost of mitigating inheritance tax or the loss of control that dealing with this tax sometimes brings, they are quite quick to change their view on this emotive subject.

There are however plenty of things you can do that have a beneficial impact on inheritance tax planning.

Make a Will

The first action anybody should take is to pop along to see their financial adviser to discuss the subject, and then see a solicitor together to speak about inheritance tax planning. Making a Will is a very good place to start.

What are the advantages of making a Will? The key advantage is that your wishes are clearly expressed and following your death the value of your estate is distributed according to your wishes.

Dying without a valid Will in place is called dying intestate and means that the value of your estate is distributed in line with an ancient law. It can also create an additional emotional burden on your family, as your wishes remain unclear.

Using a trust

Assets can be passed into a trust on your death, to both minimise inheritance tax and to control the distribution of capital or income more effectively.

This is a great alternative if you are unsure about who should receive the value of your estate or you have someone in mind but are unsure about their ability to manage large amounts of money.

Making gifts

One of the most effective ways to reduce a future inheritance tax bill is to reduce the value of your taxable estate by prudently making gifts.

An effective way to reduce the value of your estate is to transfer assets to your spouse. This is particularly useful if you have a younger or healthier spouse who is likely to outlive you!

Another type of gift is the small gift allowance of up to £250 per gift. Gifts in consideration of a marriage or Civil Partnership are also free of inheritance tax, up to £5,000 from each parent.

Everyone can make annual gifts of up to £3,000 which are free of inheritance tax. If you didn't use this gift allowance last year, you can carry it forward for a year.

Gifts made to registered charities or political parties are also free of inheritance tax.

Finally, gifts out of surplus income are free of inheritance tax. These have to be made out of income rather than capital, be part of a pattern of gifts and must not undermine your standard of living.

In conjunction, all of these gift allowances provide a good way to reduce the value of your taxable estate and consequently your inheritance tax liability. However, they do mean giving up control and ownership of assets.

If your occupation is a farmer and you are reading this, the good news in terms of inheritance tax is that agricultural relief is available to reduce the size of your taxable estate. Business property relief and woodland relief are also available.

Potentially exempt transfers

Some gifts from your taxable estate are treated as potentially exempt transfers. If you make these gifts and survive for at least seven years, the value of the gift is outside of your estate for inheritance tax purposes.

If you don't want to give up full control of assets to reduce the value of your taxable estate, you might consider using a trust.

A trust is a legal instrument which means property (any assets) transfers from the ownership of one person to the ownership of the trustees for the benefit of a group of people known as beneficiaries.

The two main types of trust are known as discretionary and absolute.
Discretionary trusts give the trustees flexibility over who benefits from trust capital and income, and when, within certain categories of beneficiaries. The wishes of the settlor can also be noted.

With an absolute trust the beneficiaries are specifically named and the gift into the trust counts as a potentially exempt transfer, which is therefore likely to be more tax efficient.

One disadvantage of using an absolute trust is that beneficiaries over the age of 18 have an immediate right to access trust assets.

Discounted gift trusts

There are several types of trust available which are well suited to inheritance tax planning. One of these which tend to be popular amongst older people is the discounted gift trust.

The gift into the trust is a potentially exempt transfer but an immediate amount of the transfer (the discount) is deemed to be outside of the estate for inheritance tax purposes.

The balance will fall outside of the taxable estate if the settlor survives seven years after making the gift. A fixed amount of the money transferred to the trust can be paid to the donor.

Keeping records

It is very important to keep accurate and detailed records in respects of any gifts you make, either capital or income.

These will help the executors deal with your estate more easily and quickly following your death as they will be able to prove to the capital taxes office that you have made certain gifts which will reduce the inheritance tax bill.

Using life assurance

Life assurance can be put in place to cover the inheritance tax bill.

This often consists of a policy on a whole of life second death basis, as the sum assured (which is equivalent to the inheritance tax bill) is payable when last surviving spouse dies.

The sum assured should be paid into a trust to keep it outside of the taxable estate and avoid aggravating the inheritance tax position.

Inheritance tax on Your Money Day

On your money day, you should consider the following steps in respect of inheritance tax.

Make sure your Will is up to date and reflects your current wishes. If it is not or does not, go and see a solicitor.

Carry out a simple calculation to determine the potential inheritance tax due on your estate by adding up the value of all assets, deducting the nil rate band and multiplying the answer by 40%.

Consider making gifts of capital or income within the available allowances and keep good records.

If you have concerns about the recipients' ability to manage money, or that assets could be lost in the future in the event of a divorce, consider a trust to retain some control over the allocation of your wealth.

Create a 'death box' which is a store of all of your relevant paperwork, including a copy of your Will and your financial adviser's business card!

Assess your advisers

"Advice is like snow – the softer it falls, the longer it dwells upon, and the deeper it sinks into the mind" – Samuel Taylor Coleridge

6pm

Financial Planning is often complicated and many people require advice.

People seek advice because they lack the time, knowledge or inclination to carry out their own financial planning, or some cases they lack all three.

Regulated advice

Financial advice in the UK is heavily regulated, with the Financial Conduct Authority (FCA) setting standards and monitoring the quality of advice being delivered.

When choosing an adviser, you should take care to make sure they are authorised and regulated by the FCA. The simplest way to do this is to check the Financial Services Register on the FCA website at www.fca.org.uk.

Qualified advisers

Individuals who provide advice in the UK need to be well qualified.

As a minimum, your adviser must hold a qualification equivalent to a Diploma standard. A commonly held qualification at this level is the Diploma in Financial Planning from the Chartered Insurance Institute.

As this is the minimum required qualification standard, many people look for an adviser who is qualified to a higher level.

Some good qualification standards to look for include Chartered Financial Planner, Certified Financial Planner or ISO 22222.

All three of these are equivalent to the first year of an undergraduate degree course, so represent a much sterner test of competence than a Diploma.

If you need advice about certain specialist subjects, your adviser should hold specific qualifications in these areas.

Two good examples are pensions and care fees planning, where the Financial Conduct Authority requires advisers to hold specific qualifications before they provide advice.

Relevant experience

In addition to qualifications, your adviser should have relevant experience. Ask them plenty of questions about the types of clients they work with and look for examples of clients who have similar objectives to your own.

Independent or restricted

Financial advice is either independent or restricted. Independent financial advice represents the gold standard of advice as it is unbiased and unrestricted, with the ability to find the best outcome for the client.

Restricted financial advice is anything which does not meet these high standards of independent financial advice.

It can be restricted in several different ways, with some restricted advisers limited to recommending products from a single product provider, which are unlikely to be the best for you as an individual.

No free lunch

When you seek advice, you should expect to pay for it. Nothing in life is free, and anything which appears at face value to be free is likely to end up costing you a lot of money in the long term!

All advisers have to disclose their charges very early in the conversation with a client. Commission can no longer be paid by product providers in respect of most types of investment, so an agreed fee known as an 'adviser charge' must instead by paid.

It is best practice for an adviser to disclose in writing to their clients exactly what they are going to do (the services they are going to provide), how much they are going to charge and how these charges are to be paid. We include these facts in an 'engagement letter' we send to all clients. You may ask your adviser to do the same.

Finding the right adviser

But how do you go about finding the financial adviser that is right for you?

It makes sense to start by asking friends, family and colleagues if they can recommend a good adviser. If someone you know has had a good experience with their financial adviser, chances are you will as well.

You should meet two or three different advisers to get to know them a little better and ask them lots of questions about their qualifications, experience and approach.

While a lot of what financial advisers do is quite similar, all approach it in a slightly different way.

You will also want to find an adviser who has a nice personality, someone you feel comfortable working with on a regular basis for a long period of time.

Remember that this might be the person you meet with once or twice a year for the next twenty or thirty years. You will need to disclose a great deal of personal and often quite sensitive information to your adviser, so make sure you feel comfortable with them.

Also find out how they deliver their services. Many financial advisers in the UK work alone, or are effectively on their own within larger companies.

Firms such as Informed Choice operate with a team approach, where various members of the team work together to construct advice and then a lead adviser is responsible for its delivery.

Different advisers will also have different investment philosophies, with some choosing to outsource their investment research and fund selection to a third party.

Think ahead

When selecting an adviser, remember to think about the service they will be providing for you in the future, as well as the advice you need today. The regular, ongoing advice you receive is likely to be just as important as the advice they provide at outset, if not more important.

Other professional advisers

Of course professional advice about your financial planning is about more than financial advisers. Two other professional advisers you might consider working with as you take control over your finances are solicitors and accountants.

Solicitors provide legal advice and other legal services which you might need at various stages of your life. We often find that our clients need to work with a private client solicitor on occasions to write a Will or administer an estate following the death of a family member.

Private client solicitors can also assist with establishing a Lasting Power of Attorney and acting as a professional trustee to help manage trust assets. In all cases, a solicitor is not mandatory and the DIY approach is possible (but may end up costing you more in the long run!).

Family lawyers are occasionally needed to help with separation and divorce, although again this is not mandatory and many people are perfectly capable of divorcing without legal assistance.

Whenever you work with a solicitor, it is important to seek financial advice at the same time if not earlier.

Your financial adviser will be able to provide the information your solicitor needs to prepare a Will or execute a Will in the most efficient way.

In respect of divorce or separation, your financial adviser can help you to value matrimonial assets and establish the most appropriate split of assets such as your pension and property.

Accountants

The other type of professional adviser you might consider is the accountant.

These advisers assist with all things tax related and are worth their weight in gold when it comes to reporting on complicated tax affairs, particularly for the self-employed.

If you find yourself in the position of needing to complete a self-assessment tax return each year, unless your income is quite simple, you might consider engaging with an accountant to help with this process.

Again, working with your accountant and financial adviser at the same time is likely to make this process much smoother and more efficient.

Your financial adviser will be able to supply your accountant with the data they need to submit tax returns, such as investment gains and details of any pension contributions you have made.

Professional adviser dream team

Your professional adviser 'dream team' therefore might consist of an independent financial adviser, solicitor (when needed) and accountant.

All three working together and pulling in the same direction can help you achieve your financial goals, dreams and objectives.

Assessing advisers on Your Money Day

What should you do on your money day in respect of assessing your advisers?

Start by asking around for recommendations in order to find a good financial adviser. Get references from people you know and trust.

Check your financial adviser is appropriately qualified and experienced. Make sure they are authorised and regulated by the FCA and get details of their charging structure in writing.

Meet your adviser and check you like them! This is going to be a lasting relationship so you need to find someone you like.

Find out what services your adviser is going to offer and ask to see examples of their work. Your adviser should be able to show you samples of their advice and review reports, as well as putting you in touch with other clients they have helped who have similar circumstances to your own.

Consider how your advice dream team might work together to help you achieve your goals.

Your annual wealth check

"The only question with wealth is, what do you do with it?" – John D. Rockefeller

This time next year

Once you've come this far, it's important to continue to manage your personal finances.

There is no sense in taking control of your finances only to let all of this hard work fall by the wayside after a year or two.

When we work with our clients, we use the following twelve point annual wealth check agenda to stimulate a conversation about their plans each year.

We have published these twelve points below as a way to encourage you to keep up the good work.

Put a date in your diary for a year from now and set aside another day as Your Money Day. In fact, it probably doesn't even need to be a full day.

Once properly addressed in the space of a day, you should be capable of giving your personal finances a quick service in the space of an hour or two, once a year.

This is time well spent.

Here is your annual wealth check.

- Update your financial situation and any changes to your financial goals and objectives.

    A lot can change over the course of the year, so get hold of updated valuations for all of your financial policies and ask yourself whether your goals in life have changed at all since you last sat down to properly consider your personal financial planning.

- Carry out a strategic review of your investment portfolio examining the asset allocation mix.

  Take a look at how your various funds are invested and consider the main investment asset classes underlying these funds, as this is what is most important from a risk and performance perspective.

- Review your underlying investment funds and examine their performance against sector averages.

  How well are your investment funds performing? If you have underperforming investment funds, there is usually no good reason to keep them in your portfolio.

- Consider making changes to your investment portfolio.

  By using the framework described in the investment chapter of this book, you can assess alternatives to the underperforming funds you currently hold and select suitable replacements.

- Review any debt you have and how that might be managed.

  Use the tips in the debt chapter of this book to understand your current debt position and make sure your plan to escape debt remains in place.

- Review your income tax, inheritance tax and capital gains tax position.
  Nobody likes paying more tax than they need to pay, so review all of these taxes, referring back to the tax and inheritance tax chapters of this book.

- Get an update on all of your pension entitlements.

  Take a look at your various sources of pension income in the future and compare these to your retirement income goals. Do you need to save more for your retirement?

- Review your estate planning, wills and power of attorney.

  If you don't yet have a will or Lasting Power of Attorney in place, make an appointment to see a solicitor and get it sorted out today. If you already have these in place, revisit them and make sure they continue to reflect your wishes.

- Review any protection plans you may have.

  If you have protection plans already in place, review the terms and premiums to make sure they remain relevant. Also consider any gap between the protection you have and the protection you need.

- Sort out all of your financial paperwork.

    You have probably received an awful lot of financial paperwork over the past twelve months, including statements and correspondence from providers and banks. Check through this, work out what you need to keep and what you can securely destroy.

- Take the wider view, including your parents and children (grandchildren).

    Financial Planning is about the bigger picture, so consider the financial needs of your parents and children, and how these might impact upon your own financial plans. Discuss care fees planning with any elderly parents.

- Update your professional advisers.

    If you have solicitors and accountants, drop them a line with an update of your current circumstances. Keep all of your professional advisers in the loop as your plans continue to develop.

www.ingramcontent.com/pod-product-compliance
Lightning Source LLC
Chambersburg PA
CBHW022020170526
45157CB00003B/1304